The Energy of the Future

WATER MOLECULE POWER REACTOR SYSTEM

Analysis of the Electron Phenomena inside the
Water Molecule Power Reactor System

The Future of Planetary and Inter Planetary Travel

CORNELIO JEREMY G. ECLE

First Edition
Innovative Research Initiative

October 2020

Dedication

The author wishes to give thanks to the Creator for making this research work possible. An enormous and significant time has been dedicated in the full completion of this research work and the efforts for this research initiative continuous through time thus, the author acknowledges the gift of time and opportunity given by the great and almighty Creator.

Table of Contents

AUTHOR'S NOTE

Innovation is a nature of mankind. Like the great Creator which created many wonders, humans also tend to create, build and amaze itself through the glorious beauty of creation. Humans as it evolved from earth have wondered in the enormous expanse of this magnificent galaxy and in itself through knowledge and understanding have tried to equal the vastness of the universe. It is the nature of humans to create things and by doing so glorifies the soul in ways indefinite. For many years great minds have written many documents which translate their understanding of things around them and through time this understanding have become a realm of knowledge for many generations. As time goes by in the present and the future, humans still do explore the universe and continue to build many different things and in fact it these things have become very complex that some ordinary humans sometimes cannot understand some of its own creations.

Knowledge and understanding have become a journey for mankind and it continues to evolve to this day.

In this book the author will explore yet another creation of mankind. The author will present a definite knowledge and understanding of a most relevant subject of this modern time, it is the subject of energy, as the modern times have evolved, the society that humans live have become exceedingly complex and complicated that it requires a source of energy to power its technology and the daily human life.

In this great generation of the digital age it has become apparent that this generation and onward is dependent on energy and in this society it cannot function properly without energy and so this modern society have invested so much resources just to make sure that the energy requirement of the community is well taken cared, of properly in the present and in foreseeable future.

Thus so energy is a vital subject to discuss upon and to invest resources as well. In fact the evolution of energy resources have evolved in the passing of time from the steam engines powered by coal to the more modern diesel engine with the use of crude oil. The discovery of nuclear fuel also contributed to development of nuclear power plant aside from the coal power plants and diesel powered plants. These energy resources however have some side effects to the environment as time elapsed such as carbon dioxide emission in the use of coal and crude oil; carbon dioxide contributes to global warming and is a direct factor in the increase of natural calamities around the planet. In the nuclear energy there is the danger of radioactive contamination and nuclear related accidents and environmental concerns. Thus to say nothing is really perfect in terms of energy concerns.

In the aftermath of these many environmental concerns toward energy production the sustainable forms of energy have risen into being. The evolution of the sustainable forms of energy have come into reality such as the wind energy, solar energy, water energy from the dams, water wave energy, and many other forms of alternative forms of energy.

One of these alternative forms of energy is the discovery that water can be transformed into its individual atomic constituents of hydrogen and oxygen respectively. And hydrogen and oxygen in gas form is a very good source of energy for use in the rocket so that the rocket can travel to the outer space from the earth's surface.

In this book it will discover the potential of water as an alternative source of fuel in the future. This book will also discuss the mathematical parameters in relation to the use of water as an alternative source of fuel in the future like it was mentioned before no energy source is perfect thus this book will also discuss the dangers and potential harms associated with the use of water as an alternative source of energy. However the potential dangers associated with the use of water as an alternative form of energy can be readily addressed upon with the use of proper technology and appropriate safety measures. These concerns will be mentioned in the book as the discussion moves along.

Through rigid scientific research and international research collaborations all technological problems can be addressed properly and with the appropriate use of available knowledge and technology.

Thus the author invites the reader to discover the potential of water as a source of energy in the future and beyond.

Water Molecule Power Reactor System

*The potential alternative energy
of the future and beyond.*

CHAPTER ONE

Analysis of the Electron Phenomena inside the Water Molecule Power Reactor System

This chapter will examine the fundamental mathematical structure of the electron phenomena inside the Water Molecule Power Reactor System.

In the design of the Water Molecule Power Reactor System there are many parameters and elements to be considered such as the physical design structure and the analysis of mathematical elements and principles which is essential and needed in order to be able to create a safe and fully working Water Molecule Power Reactor System.

In this paper it will examine the molecular level of these design principles and the mathematical theories beyond the concept of the design parameters.

There are many questions which need to be answered which are the reason the answers to those questions will be reflected in this paper and to answer those queries this paper will focus on the molecular properties of matter with respect to electrons and atoms. This paper will address one by one and tackle these mathematical problems and answer them in a way that is simple and straight forward for the readers to be able to understand. The following questions will be answered in this paper such as the unit conversion of one liter to one kilogram, what is the atomic weight of hydrogen and oxygen atom, what is the mass weight of one molecule of water, the atomic properties of hydrogen and oxygen atoms, the relationship of coulombs to ampere, how many electrons are there in one molecule of water, the ratio of electrons in terms of molecular weight and voltage and the last part is the explanation of the rate of change with respect to time.

The basic structural design and mathematical principles of a Water Molecule Power Reactor System will be illustrated and examined in this paper. All the mathematical principles and inner working theories which constitute the overall design concept of the Water Molecule Power Reactor System will be explained in a simple way. This mathematical and physical concept is vital to the overall efficiency and reliability of the proposed design, which is why in this paper it will discuss these fundamental mathematical principles one by one at a time so that it can layout the foundation of the state of the art Water Molecule Power Reactor System.

Again not all principles of mathematics and physics will be discussed on this paper only those which are relevant at the moment in time. This research constitutes many development stages and each stage brings forth new ideas and new discoveries. Although this research have now reached the second level of its design concepts there are still many ideas which still needs

3

considerable detailed and well explained data tabulations and some will be covered in this paper, but not all, only those which are relevant at this time.

And so, to begin the discussion with the first topics as shown below,

The formulas used in this book and the following formulas are based on the books from the University Physics (Young and Freedman, 2002) and College Chemistry (King, Caldwell and Williams, 1977).

1.   Unit Conversion Principles

The first topic of great interest is the discussion in the very basic and the most fundamental, in any scientific undertaking which is the unit conversion of entities such as the question of how many kilograms are there in one liter of water. Water is a very essential component of this research so that it will be mentioned more often in this paper, thus it says that one liter of water is equal to one kilogram of mass in numerical and mathematical form we have, according to Physics,

1000 milliliter of pure water $=$ 1000 grams of pure H2O gas;

$$(1.0)$$

1000 mL of H2O (liquid) $=$ 1000 g of H2O (gas);   (1.1)

1000 mL $=$ 1 Liter;   (1.2)

1 Liter of H2O (liquid) $=$ 1 kg of H2O (gas);   (1.3)

Thus it has now been shown that the relationship of one liter of liquid water and that of one kilogram of hydrogen and oxygen gas combined is as shown.

1 Liter of H2O (liquid) = 1 kg of H2O (gas);   (1.3a)

One liter of pure water molecule is the standard of measure of this research, so that it would be easy to quantity future applications with one liter of pure water as a reference base. This standard of measure would become the proposed standard quantitative value for any future technical studies in a large industrial scale development of the Water Molecule Power Reactor System.

2.   Atomic Weight of Hydrogen and Oxygen Atoms

At this point in time it would be prudent to know the atomic weight of the hydrogen and oxygen atoms which are inside the molecule of water.

Thus to say, according to Chemistry,

1 mole of water is equal to18.01528 grams/mol   (2.0)

1 mole of water = 2 grams (for 2 moles of H atoms) + 16 grams (for 1 mole of O atom) = 18 grams/mole in total;

                              (2.1)

The atomic weight of the hydrogen and oxygen atoms is important on this study for it would determine the relative weight of the hydrogen and oxygen gas produced in the Water Molecule Power Reactor.

Based on this papers scientific conclusion one liter of pure water would produce one kilogram of pure hydrogen and oxygen gas.

And now to move along with the discussion this paper, will examine another subject of great interest as follows.

3.   Mass Weight of One Molecule of Water

In the above and previous statements, it was able to determine and illustrate; the individual and combined atomic weight of the hydrogen and oxygen atom. And now this paper would need to determine the mass weight of one molecule of water, this value will be essential on the later computation of the quantity of electrons per one molecule of water.

Thus to begin with, this paper will use some of the following formula in physics, which is as follows, according to Physics,

$$M = N_A\, m; \qquad\qquad\qquad (3.0)$$

Where;

       M = molar mass, atomic weight, molecular weight;

$NA = 6.0221367(36) \times 10^{23}$ molecules/mole (Avogadro's number);

$m(H2O) =$ mass of a single molecule of water;

Now if $M = 18$ grams/mole then, $\qquad\qquad$ (3.1)

$M = NA\ m(H2O)$; $\qquad\qquad$ (3.2)

18 grams/mole $= [6.0221367(36) \times 10^{23}$ molecules]/mole $m(H2O)$;

$m(H2O) = (18$ grams/mole$)/[\ 6.0221367(36) \times 10^{23}$ molecules/mole];

$m(H2O) = 2.988972 \times 10^{-23}$ grams/molecule of H2O; $\qquad$ (3.3)

The above computed values and quantities is the value of the mass weight of one molecule of water which is composed of two atoms of hydrogen and one atom of oxygen and their combine molecular weight is $m(H2O) = 2.988972 \times 10^{-23}$ grams/molecule of H2O.

And now moving along with the discussion the next quantity to be examined is as follows,

4.   Atomic Properties of Hydrogen and Oxygen Atoms

A very important part of the design parameters, is the atomic properties of hydrogen and oxygen as being the prime source of energy originating from the water molecule. In this paper, it will try to gather all relevant technical data on hydrogen and oxygen as being the principal elements in the Water Molecule Power Reactor. Therefore it is very essential that this paper illustrate every detail that concerns the hydrogen and oxygen atoms so that it will become the ultimate guide as this writing endeavor in creating the energy of the future through the development of the Water Molecule Power Reactor System. And so the following table illustrates these quantities as shown

Table 1: Atomic Properties of Hydrogen and Oxygen Atom

Element Symbol	Atomic Number (e⁻)	Atomic Mass	Electro Negativity	Density	Melting Point	Boiling Point
O	8	15.999 g.mol⁻¹	3.5	1.429 kg/m³ at 20°C	-219 °C	-183 °C
H	1	1.007825 g.mol⁻¹	2.1	0.0899 x10⁻³ g.cm⁻³ at 20°C	-259 °C	-252.8 °C

The above Table 1, describes, that the Atomic Number this Atomic Number is also the number of electrons in a given atom, this guidance is important as the discussion of the properties of the molecule of water moves along. Also the atomic mass number indicates the mass weight of a given atom per mole.

And now to discuss these principles it can be shown that, the molecular weight of water when the water is one liter it shows as follows,

One liter of water is the proposed standard of measure of this miniature scale study and it will also be used as the basic standard in the industrial scale application of the proposed design of the Water Molecule Power Reactor System.

And so to begin with, again from the formula in Physics,

$$M = N_A\, m; \qquad\qquad\qquad (4.0)$$

Where;

M = molar mass, atomic weight, molecular weight;

N_A = 6.0221367(36) $\times 10^{23}$ molecules/mole (Avogadro's Number);

$m\,(H_2O)$ = mass of a single molecule of water;

At this point in time the value of $m\,(H_2O)$ = 1000 grams, where in,

$$M = N_A\, m; \qquad\qquad\qquad (4.1)$$

M = [6.0221367(36) $\times 10^{23}$ molecules] / [(1000 grams) / (18 grams/mole)];

M = 3.346 $\times 10^{25}$ molecules of atoms in one liter of

water; $\qquad\qquad\qquad (4.2)$

And so therefore the molar mass of one liter of water is M = 3.346$\times 10^{25}$ molecules of atoms in one liter of water, according to

9

chemistry this quantity should be multiplied by how many atoms each one molecule of matter is composed of, and in this case water is composed of three atoms per one molecule of water, which is two hydrogen atom and one atom of oxygen.

And so from the above value of M, it is said that this value of M must be multiplied by a quantity value of three and so,

$M = 3.346 \times 10^{25}$ molecules of atoms in one liter of water;

$$(4.2a)$$

$M (H2O) = M \times$ (No. of Atoms in one molecule of Water);

$M (H2O) = [3.346 \times 10^{25}$ molecules of atoms] x [3 atoms per one molecule]; $\hspace{2cm} (4.3)$

$M (H2O) = 1.0038 \times 10^{26}$ molecules of atoms in one liter of water with three atoms per one molecule of water. $\hspace{1cm} (4.4)$

Now to specify the conversion of 1000 grams of H2O to moles we have the following equations.

(1000 grams of H2O) x (1 mole of H2O/18 grams of h2O) = 55.556 moles of H2O; $\hspace{2cm} (4.5)$

At this point the quantitative volume of molecules of all atoms in one liter of water, have now been identified and was computed completely as shown above in the quantity figure of M (H2O) = 1.0038×10^{26} molecules of atoms in one liter of pure water.

The quantity of atoms per one liter of pure water is very important on the computation on the rate of change with respect to time wherein this paper will be able to calculate on how much water will be consumed in the electrolysis process and in what specific period of time will it be totally depleted, this paper will discuss this later as the discussion moves along as follows.

5.   Relationship of Ampere, Coulombs and Seconds.

Ampere is directly proportional to the coulombs and inversely proportional to time or seconds and in mathematical form we have as follows, according to Physics,

$$1 A = 1 C / 1 T \text{ (second)}; \qquad\qquad (5.0)$$

Where:

  A = amperes;

  C = coulombs;

  T = time (seconds);

Also ampere is the unit value of current and current is a quantity of the flow of electricity into a given medium. From the Ohm's Law we have,

$$I = V / R;\qquad\qquad(5.1)$$

Where:

I = current, amperes (A);

V = voltage, volts (V);

R = resistance, ohms (Ω);

And now this paper will try to compute on how many electrons are there in one volt of energy.

From Physics, it can be shown to have the following value,

$$1 \text{ coulomb} = 6.25 \times 10^{18} \text{ electrons};\qquad\qquad(5.2)$$

Therefore this paper can say that in one coulomb of charge there is a corresponding quantity of electrons which is 6.25×10^{18} electrons. Wow this is an amazing number. This paper was able to quantity the number of electrons in a charge. Thus,

$$1 \text{ coulomb} = 6.25 \times 10^{18} \text{ electrons present};\qquad\qquad(5.2a)$$

Therefore we can also say that,

1.6×10^{-19} coulomb $= 1$ electron (e^-); $\hspace{4cm}$ (5.3)

The above value, clearly illustrates the significant quantity of electrons that is present in one single charge of coulomb.

This quantity is very important in this paper's desire to be able to calculate the quantity of electrons that is present in one volt of electrical energy. By understanding the quantitative figure of electrons this paper can compare the quantity of atoms to that of the quantity of electrons. In this way this paper is able to compute the rate of change with respect to time.

From the previous research undertaken prior to this writing it was written and identified that the value of resistance to the water molecule was as follows.

Table 2: Electrical Properties of the Water Molecule Reactor (800 mL)

Type of Reactor Rods	Number of Rods in the Anode (+)	Number of Rods in the Cathode (-)	Total Resistance of the Reactor (800mL H_2O)	Total Current Requirement of the Reactor	Total Voltage Requirement of the Reactor	Power Requirement of the Reactor
Stainless Steel	4 Rods	4 Rods	40 ohms	0.3 Amperes	12 Volts DC	3.6 Watts

Assuming that the value of resistance would increase in reference to the table above Table 2, then if the quantity of water increases to 1000 ml from its previous quantity of 800 ml then the resistance would also increase from 40 ohms to 50 ohms, in the above table every 200 ml increase of water quantity would also increase the resistance by 10 ohms.

Table 3: Electrical Properties of the Water Molecule Reactor (1000 mL)

Type of Reactor Rods	Number of Rods in the Anode (+)	Number of Rods in the Cathode (-)	Total Resistance of the Reactor (1000mL H2O)	Total Current Requirement of the Reactor	Total Voltage Requirement of the Reactor	Power Requirement of the Reactor
Stainless Steel	4 Rods	4 Rods	50 ohms	0.24 Amperes	12 Volts DC	2.88 Watts

For this reason from 40 ohms it was scientifically assumed that it will increase to 50 ohms if a quantity of additional 200 ml of water is added into the Water Molecule Power Reactor.

The table above which is Table 3, now reflects the new value of resistance with respect to a 1000 ml of water quantity added, and is now present inside the proposed Water Molecule Power Reactor.

Based on Table 3, the value of current inside the Water Molecule Power Reactor is now equal to 0.24 amperes. Therefore in mathematical form it can be shown that,

$I = 0.24$ Amperes, at 1000 mL of pure

H_2O molecule; $\qquad\qquad$ (5.4)

From,

$$1\,A = 1\,C\,/\,1\,T\,(second); \qquad\qquad (5.5)$$

Therefore if the current value is equal to 0.24 A, then this computation can be shown as follows, according to Physics,

$$1 \text{ coulomb} = 6.25 \times 10^{18} \text{ electrons;} \qquad (5.5a)$$

And,

$$I \text{ (current)} = 0.24 \text{ A;} \qquad (5.6)$$

Then this paper shall convert this value of current to the corresponding number of electrons in a given current quantity; this paper shall use the following conversion process,

$$I \text{ (amperes)} = I \text{ (given current, A)} \times (6.25 \times 10^{18} \text{ electrons/ 1A);}$$

$$= (0.24A) \times (6.25 \times 10^{18} \text{ electrons/ 1A);}$$

$$I \text{ (amperes)} = 1.5 \times 10^{18} \text{ electrons / per second;} \qquad (5.7)$$

Therefore the value which is $I = 1.5 \times 10^{18}$ electrons / per second, is the quantity of electrons that will travel to a 50 ohms medium in every second.

From,

$$I = V / R; \qquad (5.8)$$

$$V = I R; \qquad (5.9)$$

Then,

$$V = IR;$$

$$V = (1.5 \times 10^{18} \text{ electrons} / \text{s}) \times (50 \text{ ohms});$$

$$V = 7.5 \times 10^{19} \text{ electron volts per second;} \qquad (5.9a)$$

The value of $V = 7.5 \times 10^{19}$ electron volts per second, is the required quantity of electrons that will travel to a 50 ohms resistance with the current of 0.24 Amperes and a voltage of 12 volts DC in every second.

Now let this paper, convert the above value into hour, as follows,

$$60 \text{ seconds} \times 60 \text{ minutes} = 3600 \text{ seconds} = 1 \text{hour;} \qquad (5.9b)$$

$$V(e^-) = (7.5 \times 10^{19} \text{ electron volts} / \text{seconds}) \times (3600 \text{ seconds} / 1 \text{ hour});$$

$$V(e^-) = 2.7 \times 10^{23} \text{ electron volts per hour;} \qquad (5.9c)$$

The value of $V(e^-) = 2.7 \times 10^{23}$ electron volts per hour, is the required quantity of electrons that will travel to a 50 ohms resistance with the current of 0.24 Amperes and a voltage of 12 volts DC in every one hour.

6.   Quantity of Electrons per Mole of a Pure Water Molecule

In every one molecule of water there exist a number of electrons and this is explained as follows, from Chemistry,

1 mole of water (H2O) = 10 electrons;   (6.0)

Hydrogen has 1 electron = 1 x 2 atoms H = 2 electrons in water;

Oxygen has 8 electrons = 8 x 1 atoms O = 8 electrons in water;

Thus from the above statements 2 electrons of Hydrogen plus 8 electrons of Oxygen equals 10 electrons in one molecule of water.

From,

M (H2O) = 1.0038×10^{26}, molecules of atoms in one liter of water with three atoms per one molecule of water.   (4.4)

From the above value this paper can now proceed to calculate the relative quantity of electrons present in a one liter of water molecule. This paper will simple multiply the value of M (H2O) = 1.0038×10^{26} molecules of atoms with 10 electrons per molecule of water then it can be shown that a value can be derived which is M = 1.0038×10^{27} electrons per one liter of pure water H2O, in mathematical form it can be shown to have as follows,

$N(e^-)$H2O   = M (H2O) x (10 electrons per molecule of H2O);

                = (1.0038×10^{26} atoms) x (10 electrons H2O);

$N(e^-)$H2O   = 1.0038×10^{27} electrons

per one liter H2O;   (6.1)

Thus now it can be shown that this paper have been able to compute the quantity of electrons present in a one liter of pure water molecule.

7.   Ratio of the Quantity of electrons per 12 VDC of energy to that of the Quantity of electrons per One Liter of Pure Water H2O

If this paper can be made to compute for the ration of the quantity of electrons per 12 volts DC of energy to that of the quantity of electrons per one liter of pure water H2O then this paper can create a value which is very significant to this present study at hand, so to express this in a mathematical form it can be shown to have a mathematical equation as follows, if this paper can denote the equation as follows,

$$w(t) = dQ / dT; \tag{7.0}$$

Where:

$w(t)$ = a value (H2O) which is a function of time;

dQ = a value (H2O) which is a measure of quantity;

dT = a value which is a measure of quantity with respect to time;

This mathematical representation is a computation of a certain value with respect to a certain quantity which is a function of time.

To simplify this equation this paper needs some of the derived values from the previous computations as follows.

$V(e^-) = 2.7 \times 10^{23}$ electron volts per hour; $\qquad$ (5.9c)

$N(e^-)H2O = 1.0038 \times 10^{27}$ electrons

per one liter H2O; $\qquad$ (6.1)

Then this paper needs to substitute the above values to the proposed equation as mentioned earlier, to put this in writing it can be illustrated as follows,

$w(t) = dQ / dT;$ $\qquad$ (7.0)

If this paper would substitute the values as follows,

Let $dQ = N(e^-)H2O$, and let $dT = V(e^-)$, and so,

$$w(t) = dQ \, / \, dT;$$

$$= N(e^-)H2O \, / \, V(e^-);$$

$$= (1.0038 \times 10^{27} \text{ electrons } H2O) \, / \, (2.7 \times 10^{23} \text{ electron volts } / \text{ hour});$$

$$w(t) = 3717.777 \, H2O \text{ per hour};$$

This value of $w(t) = 3717.777$ H2O per hour, represents the cycle per hour of a 2.7×10^{23} electrons to be able to fully interact with the electrons of the pure water molecule in order to be able to separate the hydrogen and oxygen atoms in the water molecule.

Thus to be able to represent the value of $w(t) = 3717.777$ H2O per hour, as a value of time for easy understanding this paper will now divide this value with the quantity of time which is 3600 minutes in one hour, to illustrate this in a mathematical form it can be shown as follows, if this paper can write the equation as follows,

$$dQ = w(t) \, / \, dT;$$

where;

$$w(t) = 3717.777 \, H2O \text{ per hour};$$

$$dT = 3600 \text{ seconds ; in which,}$$

$$dT = T(t_2) - T(t_1); \text{ time difference;}$$

where,

$T(t_2) = 3600$, and $T(t_1) = 0$; $dT = T(t_2) - T(0)$; if $T(t_1) = 0$, thus $dT = T(t_2)$;

Upon the scientific logical assumption that $T(t_2) = 3600$, is considered the standard based time of this paper computation.

If $T(t_1) = 0$, this means that no electrolysis process is taking place in the Water Molecule Power Reactor. And now substituting the values,

$$dQ = w(t) / dT;$$

$$= (3717.777 \; H2O / 1 \; hour) / (3600 \; seconds);$$

$dQ = 1.032 \; H2O$; Rate of Change of Quantity value with respect to time.

where,

$dQ = Q(t_2) - Q(t_1)$; Quantity difference with respect to time;

and

$Q(t_2) = 0$, the water in the reactor is fully depleted after one hour of elapsed electrolysis time,

$Q(t_1) = 1.032$, the water in the reactor is still 1 liter in quantity with zero electrolysis elapse time.

Therefore from the above values the time it takes for one liter of water inside the Water Molecule Power Reactor System, to be fully depleted will be approximately 1.032 hours from the start of electrolysis process with a 12 volts DC energy source.

This value of 1.032 hours is based on a 3.125 percent water additive of Potassium Hydroxide from the total pure water volume of 1 liter of the water fuel and Potassium Hydroxide.

The Potassium Hydroxide can also be replaced by sea water as another source of fuel for the Water Molecule Power Reactor System, however the use of sea water as a fuel for the Water Molecule Power Reactor System will now include various natural compound filters to eliminate the unwanted gas by product of chlorine gas if sea water is used for in the electrolysis process. The subject of the natural compound filters for the sea water as a fuel for the Water Molecule Power Reactor System is not thoroughly discussed in this paper they are elaborated in the next research paper after this one.

Simply to say the computations is directly dependent on the resistance of water any change in the variables with respect to the electrical properties of water will automatically make changes in the output of the computation either increasing and decreasing in value and favorable or not favorable to the proposed design of the Water Molecule Power Reactor System.

Therefore this paper can safely say that in the final conclusion it takes approximately 1.032 hours to be able to totally deplete 1 liter of pure water inside a Water Molecule Power Reactor System with an electrolysis process modification of adding 3.125 percent potassium hydroxide into the overall pure water volume of 1 liter.

The derived value of 1.032 hours is computed for water with a potassium hydroxide conductivity additive and not using sea water as a fuel for the Water Molecule Power Reactor System, the computation for the sea water fuel is very similar in nature as compared to computation as mentioned in this paper.

Thus before one hour the water level must be maintained in the Water Molecule Power Reactor System so that the Water Molecule Power Reactor can continue to produce hydrogen and oxygen gas. This gas is essential to the proposed intended production of electricity as a final product of the Water Molecule Power Reactor System.

CHAPTER TWO

Mathematical Parameters

> *This chapter will illustrate the currently known and defined mathematical parameters in relation to the design of the Water Molecule Power Reactor System.*

3.1 Ohm's Law Equation

Some formulas which the, authors have used in order to arrive into the tabulated data will be discussed in this section the first formula which have been utilized is the formula of Ohm's Law.

According to Physics the current is directly proportional to the voltage but inversely proportional to the resistance which is in the mathematical form, it can be shown as follows, according to University Physics (Young and Freedman, 2002),

$$I = V/R; \qquad\qquad (3.1.1)$$

Where;

I = Current, Amperes (A);

V = Voltage, Volts (V);

$$R = \text{Resistance, Ohms } (\Omega);$$

Another formula is the formula of power, power is directly proportional to the voltage raised to the power of two and inversely proportional to the resistance, in a mathematical equation we have,

$$P = V^2/R; \qquad\qquad\qquad (3.1.2)$$

Where;

$$P = \text{Power, Watts (W)};$$

$$V = \text{Voltage, Volts (V)};$$

$$R = \text{Resistance, Ohms } (\Omega);$$

Furthermore, speaking of mathematics the, researcher shall say that one mathematical parameters that have not been discussed on this paper is the temperature, because as the process of electrolysis is in its peak and the supply of current into the Water Molecule Reactor is steady and constant the water inside the reactor produces heat normally due to the increase in the electron activity on the water. This heat is a product of the increased and very active intermolecular interactions of the electrons and atoms inside the reactor.

The formulas used in this book and the following formulas are based on the books from the University Physics (Young and Freedman, 2002) and College Chemistry (King, Caldwell and Williams, 1977).

3.2 Quantity of Heat Equation

This heat also needs to be managed so that it will not affect the overall performance of the reactor although in the miniature skill this heat is manageable in an industrial scale that might create some technical problems, this can be addressed by introducing cooling systems into the reactor.

The technical data on temperature with respect to voltage, resistance, current and power is not presented on this paper this type of data will be discussed in the next article which the author will publish after this one.

To illustrate the formula of heat according to Physics and Chemistry, the author, shall now say that Heat in mathematical equation is equal to, according to Physics,

$$Q = mc\,\Delta T; \tag{3.2.1}$$

Where;

Q = quantity of heat;

c = specific heat capacity of an specific material;

m = mass (kg);

$\Delta T = (T_2 - T_1)$ is the difference on the change of temperature from T_1 to T_2, respectively.

In this research the author can compute the quantity of heat by putting into consideration that T_1 = the temperature of water under normal room temperature and T_2 = the temperature of the water in the reactor after a finite time in full operation. The unit for the temperature in this research is in degree Celsius ($C°$).

And the specific heat capacity of water is 4190 J/kg.K or 1Cal/g.C°. The capital letter K denotes for Kelvin named from the British physicist Lord Kelvin (1824-1907) [1], where the value of Kelvin is equal to as follows, according to Physics,

$$0\ K = -273.15\ °C \text{ and } 273.15\ K = 0\ °C \qquad (3.2.2)$$

$$T\ (Kelvin) = T\ (Celsius) + 273.15 \qquad (3.2.3)$$

3.3 Work Equation

Now one might wonder on how all this equation on the quantity of heat would relate into the present research, to answer this question the author would again examine another formula which will bring the readers closer into the equation of moving electrons in a given medium and this motion produce heat. The equation that the author, wish to look into is the equation of work. Work is mathematically presented by the following equation, according to Physics,

$$W = F \, s; \tag{3.3.1}$$

Where;

W = Work, Joule (J);

F = Force, Newton (N);

s = displacement, Meter (m);

3.4 Kinetic Energy Equation

Since the movement of the electrons inside the reactor is sporadic and nonlinear this paper will now examine the more appropriate formula which is the kinetic energy of a particle in motion. To state this formula of kinetic energy let it say, and put this into writing such as, according to Physics,

$$K = \tfrac{1}{2} mv^2; \qquad\qquad\qquad\qquad (3.4.1)$$

Where;

K = Kinetic Energy, Joules (J);

M = mass, Kg (kg);

v = velocity, meters per second squared (m/s^2);

The above equation of kinetic energy brings one closer into the kinetic energy of a moving particle and now the authors will, wish to examine how heat is produced in a particle that is moving at a definite velocity. Since water is composed of hydrogen atom and oxygen atom one might need to examine a formula which is focused on the molecular scale level of study and this can be answered through the study of physics particularly on the Molecular Properties of Matter. In the molecular properties of matter it describes to the readers the, internal properties of matter that contributes to how matter interacts to each other in the molecular level and the properties underlying the existences of matter itself. Therefore the author shall now begin the discussion with the formula of molar mass which will be discussed as follows

3.5 Molar Mass Equation

Thus one will now examine another formula which is the formula of molar mass of any substance which is denoted by letter M and the quantity M is sometimes called molecular weight, however molar mass is mostly preferred, thus one may say in mathematical form, according to Physics,

$$m = nM; \qquad\qquad (3.5.1)$$

Where;

m = total mass of the material;

M = Molecular weight or Molar mass;

n = number of moles;

The above equation is very important in this research because when one is talking about the atoms of hydrogen and oxygen. For instance the atomic weights or the atomic mass unit abbreviated amu, which is defined in Chemistry, that as 1/12 weight of one atom of the most abundant isotope of carbon which has been assigned a weight of 12 amu [3], according to Chemistry.

Furthermore also from Chemistry , it says that a mole is defined as the amount of a substance that contains as many elementary entities as there are atoms in exactly 12 grams of standard carbon-12 (^{12}C). This number of atoms has been determined experimentally to be equal to 6.022×10^{23} and it is known as the

Avogadro's number (N) in honor of the Italian physicist Amadeo Avogadro.

According to Chemistry, a molecule is defined to be as a union of two or more atoms and this constitute to a single compound. In this study the molecule which the, authors are very interested is the molecule of water which is of course composed of two atoms of hydrogen (2 x 1 amu) and one atom of oxygen (1 x 16 amu) therefore the molecular weight of water is 18 amu (u) or atomic mass unit (u) [3]. The atomic weight of hydrogen is 1 amu and the atomic weight of oxygen is 16 amu or grams/mole, from, Chemistry.

The above definitions may seem very complex at this point and so one shall now look and point ones attention to physics. This paper will now examine the principles of physics in the areas of the molecular properties of matter and it says that.

One mole of any pure chemical element or compound contains a definite number of molecules, the same number for all elements and compounds.

Additionally it says that the number of molecules in a mole is called Avogadro's number and denoted by NA. The current best numerical value of NA is, according to Physics.

$$NA = 6.0221367(36) \times 10^{23} \text{ molecules/mole;} \qquad (3.5.2)$$

Also it says in physics that the molar mass M of a compound is the mass of one mole. This is equal to the mass m of a single molecule multiplied by Avogadro's number as follows, according to Physics,

$$M = NA \ m; \hspace{4cm} (3.5.3)$$

Where;

M = molar mass, atomic weight, molecular weight;

NA = 6.0221367(36) x 10^{23} molecules/mole (Avogadro's number);

m = mass of a single molecule;

Now therefore one, have been able to illustrate the molecular weight of matter.

And matter as it is defined is anything which occupies a space, so in this article if the, researchers would wish to consider matter it will consider it to be the electrons that move around the water as the process of electrolysis in on going and is in active state.

3.6 Forces of Two Point Charges Equation

The author shall elaborate more clearly on this as the researchers move along with the discussion. With this idea the authors shall now show the mathematical formula between two point charges as follows, according to Physics,

$$F = (1/4\pi\epsilon_o)\,(q1q2/r^2); \qquad (3.6.1)$$

Where;

F = Force between two point charges;

ϵ_o = permittivity of free space;

$q1$ = charge 1;

$q2$ = charge 2;

r = measured distance between the charges;

The formula between two point charges explains the interactive energy potential between two electrons interacting along the water inside the water molecule reactor and this interaction produces heat in the water.

And now moving along with the subject of heat one shall examine the formula of Heat Current in Conduction because this is an essential element into the present study. The intermolecular interaction of matter through conduction creates friction and this friction creates and produces a significant amount of energy which is heat and this heat needs to be understood and managed properly so that one can minimize the amount of heat produced in the proposed reactor so that the reactor can also continue to produce an output of the proposed system safely and intelligently.

3.7 Heat Current in Conduction Equation

To elaborate Heat Current in Conduction one shall write this in the following mathematical form, according to University Physics (Young and Freedman, 2002) it says,

$$H = dQ/dT; \tag{3.7.1}$$

Where;

H = Heat Current;

dQ = Quantity of Heat Transferred;

dT = Temperature Difference;

Also the above formula can also be written in the following form as shown,

$$H = kA (TH - TC) / L; \hspace{3cm} (3.7.2)$$

Where;

H = Heat Current;

k = thermal conductivity, (W/m.K), (1 W = 1 J/s);

A = Cross Section Area of the rod;

$(TH - TC)$ = Temperature Difference;

L = Length of the rod;

In the above equation it states the heat conduction properties of a single conductor rod and between the conductor rods inside in the water molecule reactor.

Thus now the, author have stated a number of principles that pertains to heat and now at this point in time one will now examine heat as it applies to electricity and to a certain electronic component.

The electronic component that the author wish to study of course is the Water Molecule Reactor System as being a system that is powered by electricity and thus the author will therefore state the formula of what level of temperature range can an electronic component still operate and function properly, thus the formula is as follows, according to Physics,

$$P = (Tec - Tamb) / rth ; \qquad\qquad (3.7.3)$$

Where;

P = Highest Power Level at which a electronic component can still operate;

Tec = Maximum Allowable Temperature of the Electronic Component;

Tamb = Ambient Temperature;

Rth = is the quantity of heat or temperature (Kelvin) that an electronic component can handle per watt, (K/W);

Thus now the researcher can compute the maximum allowable temperature that the Water Molecule Reactor System can still accommodate and for the reactor to still safely operate, however with this data on mind one can manage the heat inside the reactor and integrate cooling systems to significantly reduce heat.

Additionally, another data not included on this paper is the rate of conversion process of water into its individual gas state of hydrogen and oxygen respectively. When one says the rate of conversion process what the researcher simply mean is that how many water is consumed in a given reaction process and the time factor in this given process.

In calculus it says that the rate of change with respect to time. So therefore the rate of change with respect to time in this process is not discussed on this paper again they will be explained in the next article after this one.

The rate of change with respect to time is a very important factor in the analysis of the input, process and output of this proposed research in terms of productivity, power output and management.

Safety Precautions

The computations presented in this research are experimental in nature with reference to actual experimentations conducted in a safe experimental laboratory with apparatus and devices developed and produced by the researcher.

The data and results derived from this computation were derived through careful considerations about safety, environmental precautions and meticulous planning.

Please consider safety if you are considering repeating the data on this research. Hydrogen and Oxygen gas are explosive and unstable gases if ignited and excited with an open flame or fire.

You are advised not to repeat the procedures mentioned in this research for your safety and well-being.

References

(1)   Young and Freedman. *University Physics with Modern Physics*. 10th Edition. Singapore: Pearson Education Asia Pte. Ltd. 2002.

(2)   Johnson, Johnson, Hilburn. *Electric Circuit Analysis*. 2nd Edition. New Jersey: Prentice Hall, 1992.

(3)   King, Caldwell, Williams. *College Chemistry*. 7th Edition. New York: Litton Educational Publishing, Inc. 1977.

(4)   Webster's Dictionary. *Webster's Universal Dictionary and Thesaurus*. Scotland: Geddes & Grosset 2002.

Cornelio Jeremy G. Ecle, is a University Instructor at Eastern Samar State University, Salcedo Campus, Salcedo Eastern Samar, Philippines. He has been teaching in the university since 2012.

He is a graduate of Bachelor of Science in Electronics Communications Engineering from Cebu Institute of Technology University, Cebu City, Philippines.

He also has a full pledge Masters in Information Technology from Asian Development Foundation College, Tacloban City, Philippines,

He was also a CHED Faculty Development Program II university faculty scholar.

For your research related questions please email at jeremyecle2015@yahoo.com.

www.ingramcontent.com/pod-product-compliance
Lightning Source LLC
Chambersburg PA
CBHW061530250726
48657CB00005B/2164